Entropy and Syntropy

From mechanical to life sciences

Antonella Vannini

www.sintropia.it

CONTENTS

This work describes how the concept of time and the correlated concept of causation evolved during the last centuries: the way we look at time and causation has important implications on the way we do science and on the tools we choose to use.

1

MECHANICAL CAUSALITY
AND NEWTON'S UNIVERSE:
THE LIFE-MACHINE MODEL

During the fifteen and sixteen centuries, the scientific revolution radically changed the concept of the universe which humanity had embraced during the Middle Ages, and opened the way to the understandings that we now have of the world.

The first signs of the scientific revolution can be traced back to the astronomical observations of Nicholaus Copernicus (1473-1543), who put the Sun at the center of the universe and showed the contradictions of the geocentric system, in which the Earth was placed at the center of the universe, and was based on the Aristotelian system.

The Aristotelian system was introduced by Aristotle in the fourth century B.C., and perfected by Ptolemy in the second century A.D.. According to this system, the Earth sits at the center of the universe and the Sun, Moon, Mercury, Venus, Jupiter and Saturn turn around it in circular orbits, each using a different sphere. These spheres were contained within a greater sphere of the fixed stars, behind which was the sphere of God.

The new system proposed by Copernicus, which represented a huge innovation in the astronomical field, was heliocentric, it placed the Sun at the center of the universe, around which the planets Mercury, Venus, Earth, Mars, Jupiter and Saturn all orbit, while the Moon orbits the Earth and the stars are considered to be still.

Copernicus was followed by Johannes Kepler (1571-1630), who, thanks to the use of astronomical tables, arrived at the formulation of the three laws of planetary motion, developing the Copernican heliocentric model into a scientific model.

The real change in the scientific approach, however, can be found in the works of Galileo Galilei (1564-1642) who, thanks to the telescope which had just been invented, was able to empirically prove the Copernicus's hypothesis, and provide the evidence that the Aristotelian-Ptolemaic cosmology was not true. In this way, Copernicus's hypothesis became the proven scientific model. The empirical approach of Galileo's work, and his use of mathematics, opened the way to the scientific revolution. The great contribution of Galileo can be found in the combination of scientific experiments and the use of mathematics. In order to use mathematics, Galileo studied the fundamental properties which could be observed and measured.

In the same years during which Galileo was working on his ingenious experiments, Francis Bacon (1561-1626) arrived at the formulation of the inductive method, deriving general conclusions from the observations of the experimental method. He became one of the major assertors of experimental methodology, courageously attacking the traditional schools of thought which were based on Aristotelian deductive logic. The Aristotelian method, starts from general laws, or postulates, and deducts empirical consequences which have to be proven; Bacon's inductive method starts from empirical evidence to arrive at general laws. In order to produce objective knowledge, Galileo's and Bacon's scientific methods separated the observer from the observed.

This approach totally transformed the nature and purpose of science. Whereas previously the purpose of science had been to understand nature and life, science's purpose was now that of controlling and manipulating nature. As Bacon said: "*Objective knowledge will give command over nature, medicine, mechanical forces, and all other aspects of the universe.*" In this perspective, the aim of science becomes that of enslaving nature, using torture to extract its secrets. We are now far away from the concept of "Mother Earth", and this concept will be totally lost when the organic concept of nature will be replaced by the mechanical concept of the world, which can be traced back to the works of Newton and Descartes.

Descartes (1596-1650) based his work on the idea that the "book of nature" had been written in mathematical characters. His aim was to reduce all physical phenomena into mathematical equations. He believed that nature could be described using simple motion equations, in which only space, position, and moment were relevant. *"Give me position and movement"*, he said, *"and I will build the universe."*

Among Descartes' greatest contributions was his Analytical Method of Reasoning, according to which any problem can be decomposed into its parts, and then reordered. This method lies at the foundation of modern science, and has been of great importance, allowing the development of scientific theories and complex technological projects.

Descartes' vision is based on the duality between two reigns, separate and independent: the reign of spirit, or res cogitans, and the reign of matter, or res extensa. This division between matter and spirit has had profound consequences on culture, leading to the division of body and mind which still puzzles science.

According to Descartes, matter and spirit are created by God, who is the creator of the exact order of nature that we see, thanks to the light of reasoning. However, in the following centuries the reference to God was omitted and reality was divided into the human sciences, linked to res cogitans, and the natural sciences, which were an expression of res extensa.

Descartes' vision described the material world as a machine which has no intentionality and no spirituality; nature functions according to mechanical laws, and every aspect of the material world can be explained on the basis of its position and movement. This mechanical vision was extended by Descartes to living organisms, in the attempt to organize a complete natural science. Plants and animals were considered simply as machines, whereas human beings were "inhabited" by a rational soul (res cogitans) linked to the body (res extensa) through the pineal gland, at the center of the brain. The human body, on the other hand, was similar to the body of an animal-machine. This highly mechanistic vision of nature was inspired by the high precision that was being achieved at the time by the technology and art of clock-making. Descartes compared animals to "clocks with mechanisms and springs" and extended this comparison to the human body, comparing a sick body to a badly build clock, and on the other hand, a healthy body to a well-constructed and perfectly functioning clock.

The scientific revolution reached its maturity in the works of Isaac Newton (1642-1728), who discovered the mathematical equations which govern mechanical motion, unifying the works of Copernicus, Kepler, Bacon, Galileo and Descartes. Kepler derived the laws of planetary motion from the astronomical tables; Galileo discovered the laws of falling bodies. Newton combined these results in a general formulation of laws which govern the solar systems, the planets, and also stones (and apples). He found that each body is attracted towards the Earth with the same force which attracts the planets to the Sun; he introduced the concepts of inertia and gravity, arriving at the famous laws which govern motion:

1. The *law of inertia* (already stated by Leonardo da Vinci and Galileo) which shows that bodies keep their movement until a force is applied to them;
2. The *law of proportionality between force and acceleration*, linking the force which is applied to a body with the mass and acceleration which is applied, following the relation: $F = ma$;
3. The *law of action and reaction*, which shows that to each action there is a corresponding similar and opposite reaction.

The importance of these laws is their universality. They were soon found to be valid throughout the solar system, which was considered to prove the mechanical model which had been proposed by Descartes.

In 1686 Newton presented his complete concept of nature and the world in the Philosophiae Naturalis Principia Mathematica (Mathematical principles of the philosophy of nature). This work is a set of definitions, propositions and demonstrations that for more than two hundred years have been considered the most exhaustive description of nature and the world.

In the Principia Newton describes the experimental method which he adopted, which he derived from the combination of the empirical-inductive method described by Bacon and the rational-deductive method described by Descartes. Newton says that experimental results have to be resumed into theories, systematic interpretations, and deductions from theories have to be proved by experiments: in the absence of one of these two aspects theories cannot be considered scientific. In this way Newton turned experimental methodology into the key element for the production of scientific theories and knowledge.

Newton's universe was the three-dimensional space of the classical Euclidean geometry: an empty space independent from what takes place in it. Time was considered absolute and not linked to the material world: time flowed relentlessly from the past to the future, through the present. In this space and absolute time, material particles, small solid and indivisible objects, were governed by mechanical laws. Newton considered these particles to be uniform, and explained the differences between types of matter as more or less thick aggregations of atoms.

In Newton's mechanics, all physical phenomena can be reduced to the movements of elementary particles caused by their reciprocal attraction: the force of gravity. The effect of gravity on a particle or on any material object is described by Newton's mathematical equations of motion, which are at the basis of mechanics. In this concept of the universe, empirical investigation could not extend to the elementary particles and the force of gravity: gravity and elementary particles were a creation of God, and could not be investigated.

In Opticks, Newton gave a clear description of how he believed God created the material world:

"*I think that God first created matter in the form of solid particles, hard and compact, indivisible and mobile, made of such dimensions and shapes, and of such properties, to be the most adaptable to the purpose he had created them for; these particles are solid, harder than any other body, so hard that they can never be consumed or broken: no force can divide what God made at the moment of creation."*

In this way, Newton completed the vision of a gigantic cosmic machine, totally governed by mechanical laws of causality: everything originates from a cause, which can be determined using mathematical laws. Thus the future can be calculated, if the initial conditions are known.

During the seventeenth and eighteenth centuries this mechanical approach was used to explain even the smallest variations in the orbits of planets, satellites and comets, tides, and whatever was linked to gravity.

The model was then extended beyond the boundaries of astronomy, and used to describe the behaviour of solids, liquids, gases, heat and sound.

2

THERMODYNAMICS
AND HEAT DEATH

During the nineteenth century, the use of Newtonian mechanics to describe the behaviour of heat lead to a new discipline: thermodynamics. This discipline, which can be traced back to the works of Boyle, Boltzmann, Clausius and Carnot, studies the behaviour of energy, of which heat is a form. Gases at the base of thermal machines were studied and the transformation of energy into work was analyzed; this lead to the discovery of three new laws:

1. The *law of conservation of energy*, which states that energy cannot be created or destroyed, but only transformed.
2. The *law of entropy*, which states that when transforming energy (for example from heat to work) part is lost to the environment. Entropy is a measure of the quantity of energy which is lost to the environment. When energy lost to the environment is distributed in a uniform way (i.e. where no differences in heat exist), a state of equilibrium is reached and it is no longer possible to transform energy into work. Entropy measures how close a system is to this state of equilibrium.
3. The *law of disorder* which states that within an isolated system entropy cannot diminish. When an isolated system reaches the highest level of entropy no further transformation can take place: the system has reached a state of equilibrium, known as heat death.

The principle of entropy (as expressed in the second law of thermodynamics) is of great importance, as it introduces into physics the idea of irreversible processes, such as that energy always moves from a state of high potential to a state of low potential, tending to a state of equilibrium.

Sir Arthur Eddington introduced the expression *"the arrow of time"*

(Eddington, 1958), showing that entropy forces events to move in one particular direction: from a situation of high potentials to one of low potentials, from past to future.

Our experience continually informs us about entropy variations, and about the irreversible process that leads to the dissipation of energy and the heat death: we see our friends becoming old and die; we see a fire losing intensity and turning into cold ashes; we see the world increasing in entropy: pollution, depleted energy sources, desertification.

The term irreversibility refers to the fact that in physical processes there is a tendency to move from order to disorder, and it is impossible to restore the previous level of order in which all energy was available: mechanical energy dissipates in the form of heat and cannot be recaptured. If we mix together hot and cold water we get tepid water, but we would never see the two liquids separate spontaneously.

The third law of thermodynamics, derived from the second law, states that the dissipation of energy is an irreversible process, since dissipated energy cannot be recaptured and used again, and that the entropy of an isolated system (which cannot receive energy or information from outside) can only increase until a state of equilibrium is reached (heat death).

The term "entropy" was first used in the middle of the eighteenth century by Rudolf Clausius, who was searching for a mathematical equation to describe the increase of entropy. Entropy is the combination of the Greek words "tropos", which means transformation or evolution, and the word "energy": it is a quantity which is used to measure the level of evolution of a physical system, but in the meantime it can be used to measure the "disorder" of a system.

Entropy is always associated with an increasing level of disorder. In an isolated physical system disorder (i.e. the homogeneous distribution of energy) increases leading to entropic heat death. Nevertheless, this seems to be contradicted by life: living systems evolve towards order, towards higher forms of organization, diversification and complexity, and can keep away from heat death.

Jacques Monod tried to explain life as the result of improbable conditions (Monod, 1974). In this way life could be considered compatible with the laws of entropy, but its survival was a continual fight against the laws of physics, which made life highly improbable.

Entropy evolves only in one direction: towards death and the elimination of any form of organization and structure. In order to become compatible with entropy, biology explains life as the consequence of highly improbable events constituted by the incidental formation of genetic codes and positive genetic variations. Entropy leads to the concept of a universe in which life is extraneous, a universe governed by laws which ignore life. Jacques Monod describes this, saying:

"If he accepts this message in its full significance, man must at last wake out of his millenary dream and discover his total solitude, his fundamental isolation. He must realize that, like a gypsy, he lives on the boundary of an alien world; a world that is deaf to his music, and as indifferent to his hopes as it is to his suffering or his crimes."

3

EINSTEIN: SPECIAL RELATIVITY AND TIME

In two articles dated 1905, Albert Einstein started two revolutionary tendencies: one was the special theory of relativity; the other was a new way to consider electromagnetic radiations, which would become the model of a new important theory of modern physics, the quantum theory of the atomic world.

Before Albert Einstein, time was thought to be absolute, whereas speed was relative. This description was known as Galileo's relativity. In order to explain it, Galileo used the example of a sailor who fires a cannon in the direction in which a ship is moving: an observer on the sea shore would see the speed of the cannon ball result from the sum of the speed of the ship plus the speed at which the ball was fired; while the sailor on the ship would see the ball moving only at the speed at which the ball was fired.

At the end of the eighteenth century Maxwell found in electromagnetism experiments that the speed of light did not add to the speed of the body which was emitting it, and Michelson and Morley proved experimentally that the speed of light was a constant: it never adds to the speed of the body which is emitting it. The profoundly innovative researches of Hendrik Lorentz, on electrodynamics and optics in moving bodies, lead to mathematical equations in which the speed of light is always constant.

Analyzing the results obtained by Michelson, Morley and Lorentz, Einstein found himself forced to invert Galileo's relativity according to which time is absolute and speed is relative; in order to describe the fact that the speed of light is constant, it was necessary to accept that time is relative.

As an example, let us imagine, after 500 years, a sailor on a very fast space ship heading towards Earth who shoots a laser light ray towards Earth. An observer on Earth would see the laser light moving at 300,000 km/s, the speed of light, but the sailor on the space ship would also see the laser ray moving at 300,000 km/s. The strange thing is that, because the space ship is moving very fast, approaching the speed of light, the sailor should see the laser ray moving at the speed of light minus the speed of the space ship, and not at 300,000 km/s.

Einstein arrived at a mathematical demonstration that what varies is not the speed of light, but time. When we move in the direction of light our time slows, and for us light continues to move at the same speed. This leads to the conclusion that approaching the speed of light time would slow down and stop, and if we could move at speeds higher than the speed of light, time would reverse.

In other words, events which happen in the direction in which we are moving become faster, because time slows down, but events which happen in the direction from which we are coming become slower, because time becomes faster.

In order to explain this situation, Einstein liked to use the example of lightning which strikes a railway simultaneously in two different points, A and B, far away from each other (Einstein, 1967).

An observer sitting on a bench half-way would see the lightning strike the two points simultaneously, but a second observer on a very fast train moving from A to B (figure 1) passing next to the first observer at the moment in which the lightning strikes the two points would have already experienced the lightning striking point B, but would have not experienced the lightning striking point A. Even if the two observers share the same point of space at the same moment, they cannot agree on the events which are happening in the direction in which the second observer is moving. Agreeing on the existence of contemporary events is therefore linked to the speed at which the observers are moving.

In other words, events which take place in the direction in which we are moving become faster, because our time slows down; but events which happen in the direction opposite to our movement become slower, because our time speeds up. It is important to note that time flows differently if the event is happening in the direction towards which we are moving, or in the direction from which we are coming; in the first case they become slower and in the second case faster:

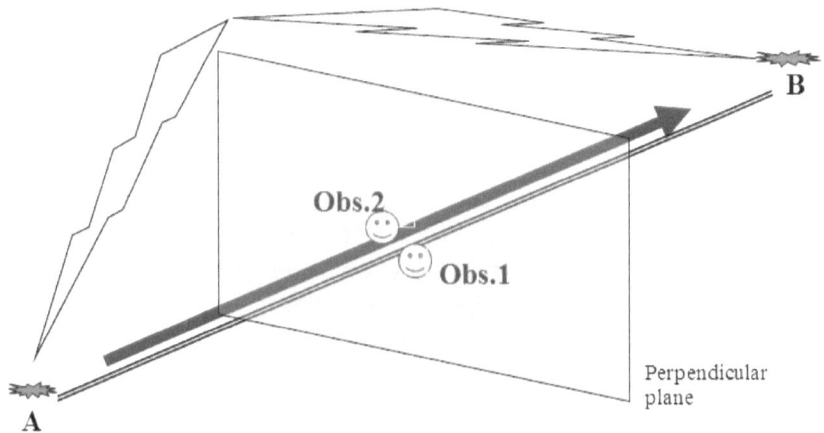

This example is limited to two observers; but what happens when we compare more than two observers moving in different directions at high speeds? The first couple (one on the bench and the other in the train) can reach an agreement only on the contemporary existence of events which happen on a plane perpendicular to the movement of the train. If we add a third observer moving in another direction, but sharing the same place and moment with the other two observers, they would agree only on events placed on a line which unites the two perpendicular planes; if we add a fourth observer, they would agree only on a point which unites the three perpendicular planes; if we add a fifth observer, who is not even sharing the same point in space, no agreement would be possible at all.

If we consider that only what happens in the same moment exists (Newton's time concept), we would be forced to conclude that reality does not exist. In order to re-establish an agreement between the different observers, and in this way the existence of reality, we need to accept the coexistence of events which could be future or past for us, but contemporary for another observer. Extending these considerations, we arrive at the necessary consequence that past, present and future coexist.

Einstein himself found it difficult to accept this consequence of special relativity, according to which past, present and future coexist; but the unified time model was perfected by Minkowski, who coined the term "chronotope" to describe the union of space and time. Since Einstein presented his theory of relativity, time has become a dimension of space: space is no longer limited to 3 dimensions. As we can move in space, so we can also move in time: space now has 4 dimensions, and is therefore named space-time.

Another important consequence of the theory of relativity is that mass is a form of energy, and even a stationary object has energy in its mass. The relation between mass and energy is expressed by the famous equation $E=mc^2$, where c is the speed of light, m the mass and e the energy. The equivalence between mass and energy opened the way to quantum mechanics, where mass is no longer associated with a material substance, but seen as a type of energy. Particles are therefore now studied according to relativity, where time and space are united in a four-dimensional continuum. Atomic particles are now considered dynamically to be forms of time-space: their space form makes them appear as objects with mass, while their time form makes them appear as waves with energy. Since the introduction of relativity, matter and its activity are two aspects which can no longer be separated: they are two forms of the same space-time unity.

In 1915 Einstein presented the "general relativity" model, in which the force of gravity was added to special relativity.

4

QUANTUM MECHANICS AND SUPERCAUSALITY

The concept of anti-matter can be dated to 1928, when Paul Dirac formulated his famous relativistic equations of the electron.

Dirac noted that the energy-momentum-mass equation had two solutions: the electron with positive energy (or retarded potentials, in which waves diverge from causes located in the past) and the electron with negative energy (or anticipated potentials, in which waves converge towards causes located in the future).

The only way to explain the anticipated potentials was to admit the existence of symmetrical particles: the positrons. These particles are identical to the electron but have an inverted flow of time: while the electron moves from the past to the future, the positron moves from the future to the past. The existence of the positron was proved empirically two years later, when Andersen demonstrated their existence in cosmic rays.

Now we know that in nature each atomic particle has a corresponding anti-particle, symmetrical in time and energy, which flows from the future to the past. Feynman, in 1949, thanks to his famous diagrams, arrived at an important generalization which can be summarized by saying that all particles move from the past to the future, while all anti-particles move from the future to the past.

In Fractals of brain, fractals of mind, it is possible to read Chris King's article "*Fractal Neurodynamics and Quantum Chaos*", in which he presents the model of "supercausality".

King starts from the energy-moment-mass equation which links energy, matter and movement:

$$e^2 = p^2 c^2 + m^2 c^4$$

This equation shows that the value of energy has two solutions:

1. the first one +*e*, with a positive sign, corresponds to positive energy in which time flows in the usual way, from past to future;
2. the second solution -*e*, with a negative sign, corresponds to negative energy in which time is inverted and flows from the future to the past.

It is well known that square-roots always give way to two solutions, one positive and one negative: this leads to the mathematical possibility of the existence of a symmetrical type of energy and time. If we put negative energy into the famous equation $E=mc2$, we get negative matter.

Einstein showed that positive matter can only tend to the speed of light, but never reach it; on the contrary, negative matter can only move at a speed higher than the speed of light, flowing, according to special relativity, from the future to the past: this situation is known as the inversion of the time arrow.

In this way, quantum mechanics arrived at a description of the universe which is symmetrical in respect of time: on one hand there is matter which moves from the past to the future, on the other hand there is anti-matter which moves from the future to the past.

This concept of the universe had its first demonstration with the discovery, by Dirac, of the anti-particle of the electron, the positron. Later Feynman generalized the existence of anti-particles to all atomic particles, while Donald Ross Hamilton showed that for each light emitter an absorber must exist, for which time flows in the opposite direction.

King outlined the contribution of Cramer, who showed that the encounter of emitters and absorbers can be used in quantum mechanics to describe the creation of photons which are the result of the interaction of past and future, of diverging and converging waves (Cramer, 1986). This constant interaction between past and future creates a paradox which cannot be solved on the basis of time determinism.

As Penrose has shown, the space-time description which is now emerging is incompatible with traditional concepts of causality and determinism (Penrose, 1989).

The fact that past and future causes coexist is named by King as "supercausality".

In this model, King uses the concept of time inversion to describe brain structures. According to King, brain structures are constantly faced with bifurcations generated by the encounter of information coming from the past (diverging waves, causes) and information coming from the future (converging waves, attractors). In each moment, brain structures have to decide which path to follow, which bifurcation.

According to King, free-will and learning are a result of this constant activity of choice, this constant indeterminism.

5

THE ROLE OF INFORMATION
THE BOOLEAN OBSERVER

Giuseppe and Salvatore Arcidiacono have shown that the equations of wave mechanics give way to two solutions: diverging waves, with causes located in the past, and converging waves, with causes located in the future (Arcidiacono, 1991). It is therefore possible to state that besides mechanical causation, another type of causation exists which Giuseppe and Salvatore Arcidiacono named final causation. This consideration leads to a description of life which is no longer linear but circular, in which both mechanical and final causation are required.

Life becomes the result of the constant interactions between causes placed in the past (diverging waves) and causes placed in the future (converging waves): the question as to whether tissues are determined by cells or cells are determined by tissues can be solved by accepting both alternatives. Life is no longer a machine, but a creative system which tends towards causes located in the future. According to Davies, science has been dominated for centuries by Newton's vision which describes the universe as a machine, but now we know that the laws of the universe are creative, and that they support evolution and innovative processes (Davies, 1974).

Similarly to King, Giuseppe and Salvatore Arcidiacono describe living systems as constantly placed in a state of choice between Boolean alternatives: between information coming from the past and information coming from the future. This constant choice is at the basis of learning and growth.

Several authors have emphasized that information reduces entropy. A typical example on how information optimizes the use of energy is provided by the first computer: Eniac. It could perform small calculations using the amount of energy which was needed by a town of 30,000 inhabitants; nowadays, computers perform calculations which are incredibly complex consuming less energy than is needed to light a small table lamp. This drastic reduction in entropy has been possible thanks to the increase in information in modern computers.

Following these considerations, Ludwig von Bertalanffy, father of the general system theory, considered information to be any element which reduces entropy, showing that information can take the form of a project, an organization, a structure, or generally a system. Bertalanffy associated information with a new quality which he named neg-entropy: negative entropy (Bertalanffy, 1977).

Léon Brillouin also associated information with neg-entropy; his deep knowledge of statistical mechanics and telecommunications gave him the chance to recognize the importance of information: he equates information and entropy, showing that a precise relation exists between the energy of a system and the information present in the system.

"Entropy is a measure of the loss of information: the higher the information, the lower the entropy. Information represents the negative term of entropy, and therefore it is possible to define information as negative entropy." (Brillouin, 1962)

Costa de Beauregard introduced the concept of information which comes from the future:

"In quantum mechanics it is possible to carry out experiments deciding only after the experiment is started which aspect of reality we want to observe. If, for example, two particles originate from a common point, we can decide later if we want to observe them as waves or as particles. Now, in an astrophysics laboratory, when we decide whether to see waves or particles of photons coming from distant quasars, we generate a backwards effect to the moment when photons were emitted, 4 billion years ago. What happened 4 billion years ago is determined by what we decide to see in our laboratory." (Beauregard, 1957).

Fred Hoyle noted that the only way to introduce concepts of order and organization in physics is to use information which comes from the future (Hoyle, 1984).

We can conclude by saying that one of the main qualities of the inversion of the time arrow is the increase in information, and, as a consequence, the reduction of entropy.

6

HOW CAN WE INTERPRET LIFE?

As we have just seen:

- Newton's physics describes life as a machine;
- Thermodynamics and entropy consider life impossible or highly improbable;
- Quantum physics describes life as a consequence of negative energy entropy and the inversion of the time arrow.

Recently, many different proposals have arisen:

- Erwin Schrödinger was looking for the nutrient which is hidden in our food, and which keeps us away from the heat death. Why do we need to eat biological food; why can we not feed directly on the chemical elements of matter? Schrödinger answered this question by saying that what we feed on is not matter but neg-entropy, which we absorb through the metabolic process (Schrödinger, 1988).
- Ilya Prigogine, winner in 1977 of the Nobel prize for chemistry, introduced in his book "*The New Alliance*", a new type of thermodynamics, the "*thermodynamics of dissipative systems*", typical of living systems. Prigogine stated that this new type of thermodynamics cannot be reduced to dynamics or thermodynamics (Prigogine, 1979).
- Hermann Haken, one of the fathers of the laser, introduced a level that he named "ordinator", which he uses to explain the principles of orders typical of the laser light (Haken, 1983).
- Teilhard de Chardin introduced the concept of radial energy, which brought him to the formulation of his "*law of complexification*" that he used to explain why biological systems evolve towards forms which are always more complex (Teilhard de Chardin, 1955).

In 1941, Luigi Fantappiè developed his well-known *"unified theory of the physical and biological worlds"*, where he demonstrated the existence of a principle which is symmetrical to entropy, which he named *"syntropy"*. The importance of his concept is due to the fact that it was introduced not in an arbitrary way, but as the consequence of quantum mechanics.

7

FANTAPPIE': A SHORT BIOGRAPHY

Luigi Fantappiè was born in Viterbo, Italy, on the 15th of September 1901.

He graduated in high mathematics at the age of 21 on the 4th of July 1922 in the most selective Italian university, the *"Scuola Normale di Pisa,"* where he was a room-mate and close friend of Enrico Fermi.

In 1926 he became professor of algebraic mathematics at the University of Florence, and in 1927 of infinitesimal analysis at the University of Palermo.

His important mathematical researches were recognized with the Mathematical Medal of the Italian Science Society in 1929, and with the prize in mathematics of the *"Accademia dei Lincei"* and with the Volta prize of the *"Accedemia d'Italia"* in 1931.

In 1931-32 he taught in the Universities of Berlin, Gottinga, Munich, Colonia, Friburgo and Lipsia, and in 1932 he became Director of the Institute of Mathematics at the University of Bologna.

After 6 years in Brazil, where he founded and directed the Mathematical Institute of San Paolo, he became vice-president of the National Institute of High Mathematics at the University of Rome (founded and directed by Francesco Severi) where he taught high mathematics analysis.

In 1954 he was nominated Accademico dei Lincei and in 1955 he was given the golden medal as Benemerito della Cultura.

He died in Bagnaia on the 28th of July 1956.

8

THE UNIFIED THEORY
OF THE PHYSICAL AND BIOLOGICAL WORLD

At the beginning of 1940, Luigi Fantappiè was working on the equations of relativistic and quantum physics when he noted that the equation of D'Alembert, which governs the propagation of waves, had two solutions:

- The solution of the *"retarded potentials"*, which describes waves diverging from a source, from causes located in the past which have produced them;
- The solution of the *"anticipated potentials"*, which describes waves converging towards a source, to a cause located in the future.

Diverging waves (for example heat, sound and radio waves) describe phenomena which are caused by the past, while waves which converge describe all those phenomena which are attracted towards causes located in the future.

What Fantappiè discovered can be considered a natural evolution of quantum mechanics:

1. In 1905, Einstein had introduced the special theory of relativity, which described the universe using four dimensions: three dimensions of space and a fourth dimension relative to time, paving the way for descriptions in which past, present and future co-exit;
2. In 1928, Dirac demonstrated the existence of the positron as an anti-particle of the electron, starting the first studies on antimatter and the inversion of time.
3. Quantum mechanics demonstrated that every physical law is symmetrical in respect of time.

Fantappiè discovered that:

- diverging waves, in which causes are located in the past, describe chemical and physical phenomena governed by the principal of entropy;
- converging waves, in which causes are located in the future, describe a new type of phenomenon, governed by a principle symmetrical to entropy which Fantappiè named syntropy.
- life is governed by the principle of syntropy, expressing finality, differentiation, order and organization.

These discoveries were presented on the 30th of October 1942 at the Accademia d'Italia, in the form of volume titled *"The Unified Theory of the Physical and Biological World"*.

9

SYNTROPY AND VITALISM

To overcome the difficulties generated by the principle of entropy, eighteen century biologists proposed the introduction of vital forces which oppose physical and chemical forces.

These vital forces would have governed living systems in different ways from physical forces.

The hypothesis was based on the fact that it had not been possible to produce living substances from inorganic matter.

But the artificial production of urea, obtained by Woehler in 1828, through organic synthesis, proved that vitalism was wrong.

Even if syntropy is a typical quality of living organisms, it is profoundly different from vitalism, as it derives naturally from physical laws.

10

SYNTROPY AND ENTROPY
COMPLEXITY AND ORDER

In Fantappiè's model, each expression of reality is described as the consequence of a particular form of interaction between entropy and syntropy. It is possible to observe 3 categories:

1. *Entropic phenomena*, in which entropic aspects prevail: their qualities are governed by the principle of entropy. As a consequence, the evolution from complex to simple and homogeneous states is observed.
2. *Syntropic phenomena*, in which syntropic aspects prevail: their qualities are governed by the principle of syntropy. As a consequence, the evolution from simple to complex and differentiated states is observed.
3. *Equilibrium phenomena*, in which the syntropic and entropic aspects reach an equilibrium: in these phenomena it is not possible to observe syntropic differentiation and entropic leveling. These phenomena are placed between determinism (causes placed in the past) and indeterminism (attractors, causes placed in the future).

Equilibrium phenomena are governed by the following principles:

1. The principle of *causality-attraction*, on the basis of which each phenomenon is the product of causes driven by attractors. As a consequence it depends not only by the past (efficient causes), but also by the future (attractors);
2. The principle of *partial reproducibility*, on the basis of which it is possible to manipulate the entropic side directly, but the syntropic side only indirectly. This means that the syntropic aspects of the universe are outside the reach of researchers;

3. The principle of *leveling-differentiation*, on the basis of which the

entropic component is subject to leveling while the syntropic component is subject to differentiation. As a consequence of each constructive process, a leveling process is associated.

Equilibrium phenomena suggest that attractors can be observed even in physical phenomena.

In 1963 the meteorologist Lorenz discovered the existence of chaotic systems which react, in each point of their states, to small variations. Studying, for example, a simple mathematical model of meteorological phenomena, Lorenz found that a small perturbation could generate a chaotic state which would amplify, making weather forecasting impossible (Lorenz, 1963).

Analyzing these unforeseeable events, Lorenz found the existence of an attractor which he named the *"chaotic attractor of Lorenz"*: this attractor causes microscopic perturbations to be amplified, and interfere with the macroscopic behaviour of the system.

Lorenz described this situation with the words: *"The flap of a butterfly's wing in Brazil can set off a Tornado in Texas."*

Lorenz's discovery started the science of chaos, which is centered on attractors.

In this regards it is interesting to note the contradiction in the way the words *"order"* and *"disorder"* are used. In thermodynamics disorder is a property of mechanical deterministic systems, governed by entropy with causes in the past, while order is a property of syntropy and attractors, in which causes are placed in the future.

In the science of chaos, on the contrary, order is associated with deterministic systems (entropic systems), while disorder is associated with attractors (syntropic systems). The origin of this contradiction can be found in the fact that in the science of chaos, "ordered" systems are those which can be predicted (a property which is true only within entropic systems), while "disordered" systems are those which cannot be predicted (a property which is true within syntropic systems).

The science of chaos links order to entropy and disorder to syntropy; but, as we have seen already, as a consequence of the second law of thermodynamics, entropy is linked to disorder and syntropy is linked to order.

The fact that syntropic phenomena are attracted by the future and cannot be predicted in a precise and mathematical way is associated at the micro-level with chaos.

It is interesting to note that the forms of order which syntropy generates at the macro-level are accompanied, at the micro-level, with chaotic / non-deterministic processes.

11

CHAOS AND FRACTALS

Fractal geometry, was discovered in the 1970's by Mandelbrot.

When inserting attractors in a geometrical system, complex and ordered figures are generated. In fractal geometry an attractor is an operation, a function which tends to a limit which will never be reached (Mandelbrot, 1987). For example, if we repeat the square-root of any positive number except one, the result will tend to one, but never reach it. The number one is therefore the attractor of the square-root of positive numbers. In the same way, if we square a number superior to one the result will tend to infinity, and if we square a number inferior to one the result will tend to zero.

Fractal figures are a result of the interaction of attractors introduced into a geometrical figure. Fractals show, in a visual way, what happens when syntropy and entropy interact together.

Fractal geometry reproduces some of the most important structures of living systems, and many researchers are arriving to the conclusion that life processes follow fractal geometry: the outline of a leaf, the growth of corals, the form of the brain and the nervous terminations.

 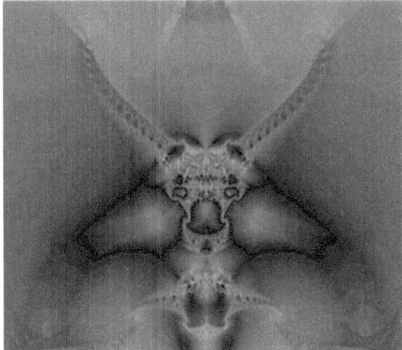

Note the similarity of these fractal images with brain structures (http://fractalarts.com/)

An incredible number of fractal structures has been discovered, for example:

1. Blood arteries and coronary veins show ramifications which are fractals. Veins divide into smaller veins which divide into smaller ones. It seems that these fractal structures have an important role in the contractions and conduction of electrical stimuli: the spectral analysis of the heart frequency shows that the normal frequency resembles a chaotic structure;
2. Neurons show fractal structures: if neurons are examined at low magnifications, ramifications can be observed from which other ramifications depart, and so on;
3. Lungs follow fractal designs which can easily be replicated with a computer. They form a tree with multiple ramifications, and with configurations which are similar at both low and high magnifications.

These observations have led to the hypothesis that the organization and evolution of living systems (tissues, nervous system, etc.) can be guided by attractors (causes placed in the future) in a similar way that which happens in fractal geometry.

Fractal structures of the human body grow in complexity following the evolution of life. Fractal structures in living organisms probably evolve through limited information which forms part of a complex algorithm, and guides living organisms in their evolution.

At present, medicine seems to be one of the leading fields in the study and development of fractal science and the science of chaos. Researchers need to understand in a deeper way how evolution is guided by attractors, and how apparently chaotic systems are part of higher forms of order. For instance, brain processes are characterized by the co-presence of chaos and order: chaos is observed at the micro-level where non-deterministic processes take place, while order is observed at the macro-level where attractors lead inevitably to an increase in syntropy.

12

QUANTUM PROCESSES IN THE BRAIN
CHAOS DYNAMICS

C. King states that *"dual-time supercausality results in pseudo-random behaviour consistent with the probability interpretation, which is non-local not only in space, but also in time. This could enable a neural net to become internally interconnected through sub-quantum effects which were non-local in time, and hence enable a form of predictivity unavailable through classical computation. The mutual exchange of quanta between such units would make them a contingent transactional set of emitters and absorbers."*

Chris King introduces the possibility of processes which are non-local in time and space. It is important to remember that the concept of non-locality derives from the inversion of the time arrow, which is a consequence of the existence of anti-particles which move faster than the speed of light (as shown in the second chapter). This inversion of the time arrow opens communication gates between points of the universe which are non-local in time and space; gates which are described by the expression time/space non-locality.

The existence of non-local processes is one of the main qualities of the inversion of the time arrow, and could be considered one of the basic qualities of syntropic processes and attractors. Living systems and brain processes are typical expressions of syntropic properties, so it is consistent to consider non-locality a quality of living systems, and in particular of brain processes.

Jeffrey Satinover in a recent book suggests that the human brain shows structures which seem perfectly designed to capture and amplify quantum effects (Satinover, 2002).

In 1948, while working on the hypothesis of quantum processes in life structures, Luigi Fantappiè suggested that the brain could act as a quantum gate in which past, present and future coexist.

As an example, Fantappiè suggested that memory, according to quantum mechanics, could use non-local processes, thereby connecting directly with distant points of space and time. When we remember past events, the brain would link to this non-local event, which is placed in the past but is still present, and the information would come directly through the link and not from "memory storage" inside the brain.

After 60 years, this incredibly suggestive hypothesis is still too courageous, but it could open new frontiers in the understanding of how the human brain and memory work.

King states that the supercausal model derived from quantum physics shows that free will is a consequence of the fact that cells are constantly forced to choose between information which comes from the past (diverging waves, emitters/entropy) and information which comes from the future (converging waves, absorbers/syntropy). This constant state of choice gives form to chaotic behaviour on which the conscious brain feeds, a process which is syntropic and not reproducible in a laboratory, or through computational techniques.

Widening psychology to non-local quantum-mechanics and to the qualities of syntropy would open the way to scientific investigations which could deal with all those topics, which modern psychology has currently kept outside its reach.

13

EPILOGUE
SCIENCE AND RELIGION, THE END OF DUALISM

The scientific revolution that was started by Newton and Galileo divided culture into two parts: on the one side science, capable of studying the entropic aspects of reality, and on the other side religion, dedicated to the syntropic aspects of reality, such as the soul and the final causes.

The introduction of syntropy into the scientific model implies a profound change in the cultural balance between science and religion, which Fantappiè describes as follow:

"Let us conclude by looking at what we can say about life. What makes life different is the presence of syntropic qualities: finalities, goals, and attractors. Now as we consider causality the essence of the entropic world, it is natural to consider finality the essence of the syntropic world. It is therefore possible to say that the essence of life is the final causes, the attractors. Living means tending to attractors. But how are these attractors experienced in human life? When a man is attracted by money we say he loves money. The attraction towards a goal is felt as love. We now see that the fundamental law of life is this: the law of love. I am not trying to be sentimental; I am just describing results which have been logically deducted from premises which are sure. It is incredible and touching that, having arrived at this point, mathematical theorems start speaking to our heart!" (Fantappiè, 1993).

The deep emotional and cultural impact, that this new vision deriving from quantum mechanics has is testified to in the works of Fritjof Capra, who describes the difficulties that Einstein had in accepting the existence of non-local connections, and the resulting importance of probability:

"This was the theme of the famous controversy between Bohr and Einstein. Einstein expressed his opposition to the Bohr's quantum interpretation with the words 'God does not play dice with the universe.' At the end of the controversy Einstein had to recognize that quantum theory, in the Bohr and Heisenberg

interpretation produced a coherent system of thought."

David Bohm, in his book on quantum theory, makes an interesting analogy between quantum processes and thought, arriving at the hypothesis that thanks to quantum mechanics, the universe starts to look more like a big thought than a big machine (Bohm, 1951).

In 1967, Ilya Prigogine, a Nobel prize winner in chemistry and an expert in complex systems thermodynamics, formulated the concept of dissipative structures which are able to avoid heat death. Prigogine introduced a new level of thought, different from mechanics or thermodynamics, that is similar to Fantappiè's syntropy. In his book *"The New Alliance"* he presented his thoughts as a new paradigm which could reunite science and religion.

Fantappiè stated that nowadays we see written in the book of nature - which Galileo said was in mathematical characters - the same laws of love that we find written in the holy books of the major religions.

"[...] the law of life is not the law of hate, the law of force, or the law of mechanical causes; this is the law of non-life, the law of death, the law of entropy; the law which dominates life is the law of finalities, the law of cooperation towards goals which are always higher, and this is true also for the lowest forms of life. In humans this law takes the form of love, since for humans living means loving, and it is important to note that these scientific results can have great consequences at all levels, particularly on the social level, which is now so confused. [...] The law of life is therefore the law of love and differentiation. It does not move towards leveling and conforming, but towards higher forms of differentiation. Each living being, whether modest or famous, has its mission, its finalities, which, in the general economy of the universe, are important, great and beautiful."

REFERENCES

- Arcidiacono G.S. Entropia, Sintropia e Informazione. Di Renzo Editore, Roma 1991.
- Bateson G. Mind and Nature. Dutton, New York 1979.
- Bertalanffy L. von. Teoria Generale dei Sistemi. ISEDI, Milano 1977.
- Bohm D. Quantum Theory. Prentice-Hall, New York 1951.
- Brillouin L. Science and information Theory. Accademic Press, New York 1962.
- Capra F. Il punto di svolta. Feltrinelli, Milano 1992.
- Cattell R.B. The scientific use of factor analysis. Plenum Press, New York 1976.
- Costa De Beauregard O. Théorie synthetique de la relatività restrinte et des quanta. Gauthier – Villars, Paris 1957.
- Cramer J.G. The transactional interpretation of quantum mechanics. Rev. Mod. Phys 1986; 58: 647 – 687.
- Davies P. The Physics of Time Asymmetry. Surrey Press, 1974.
- Eddignton A. The Nature of the Physical world. Ann Arbor Paperbacks, University of Michigan Press 1958.
- Einstein A. Relatività: esposizione divulgativa. Universale Bollati Boringhieri, Torino 1967.
- Fantappiè L. Principi di una teoria unitaria del mondo fisico e biologico. Di Renzo Editore, Roma 1991.
- Fantappiè L. Conferenze Scelte. Di Renzo Editore, Roma 1993.
- Feynman R.P. Theory of positron. Phys. Rev. 1949; 76: 749.
- Freeman W. Come pensa il cervello. Einaudi, Milano 2000.
- Haken H. Sinergetica, il segreto del successo della natura. Bollati Boringhieri, Torino 1983.
- Hoyle F. L'universo intelligente. Mondatori, Milano 1984.
- King C.C. Dual-time supercausality. Phys. Essays 1989; 2: 128 – 151.
- Lorenz E. Deterministic Nonperiodic Flow. Journal of the Atmospheric Sciences 1963; 20: 130-140.
- Mac Cormac E.R, M.I.Stamenov. Fractals of Brain, fractals of mind. In advances in counsciousness research, Vol.7, John

Benjamins Publishing Company, Amsterdam 1996.

- Mandelbrot B.B. Gli oggetti frattali. Einaudi, Torino 1987.
- Monod J. Il caso e la necessità. Oscar Mondatori, Milano 1974.
- Penrose R., Isham C. Quantum Concepts in Space & Time. Oxford University Press 1989.
- Prigogine I. La nuova alleanza. Longanesi Editore, Milano 1979.
- Prigogine I. Tempo, irreversibilità e strutture in La nuova alleanza. Longanesi Editore, Milano 1979.
- Satinover J. Il cervello quantico. Macro Edizioni, Cesena 2002.
- Schrödinger E. Che cos'è la vita. Sansoni, Firenze 1988.
- Teilhard de Chardin P. Le phénomène humain. Ed. du Seuil 1955.

BOOKS

The ASIN code is shown in brackets. It can be used to search for books if you have difficulties. The books are available in all formats. Kindle, Paper Back, Hard Cover and Audio book.

The Attractor (B0GZNHPQF9)
Introduction to Syntropy (B006QHVZPA)
Entropy and Syntropy: from mechanical to life sciences (B06XGV6XMK)
A Syntropic Model of Consciousness (B06XKKCC6F)
The balancing role of Entropy and Syntropy (B00KL4SP70)
The Unitary Theory (B01NCOVYUK)
Teilhard and Fantappiè: the converging evolution (B0H248DPN1)
Retrocausality: Experiments and Theory (B005JIN51O)
Supercausality (B005N5KLCE)
Origin of life, evolution and consciousness in the light of the law of syntropy (B005HADKWS)
The Vital Needs Theory (B006M0L0R4)
The methodology of concomitant variations (B00MOBIGWC)
World War III or Syntropy? (B0FSFC8FBT)
Apocalypse and Syntropy (B0B5RMPGKC)
Syntropy and Homeopathy (B07K5XRQNF)
Bach's flowers remedies, synchronicities and attractors (B086XBFTC1)
Climate Change (B07SRBCZVF)
Are we entering the next ice age? Will humanity survive? (B071FQLX6Z)
Syntropy the Trilogy (B09SQ5DNN7)
Money (B07S3TTS7J)
Depression (B07XGHWZ9G)
Liquidarism, Syntropy and Vital Needs (B07QDGZWPS)
Syntropy, Precognition and Retrocausality (B074W7ZL3J)
The invisible force of love (B01I4S8KV0)
The Path to Happiness (B071YWSK6K)
Colonization of Mars, Ice Age, Biological Teleportation and the Meaning of Life (B095PX92H7)